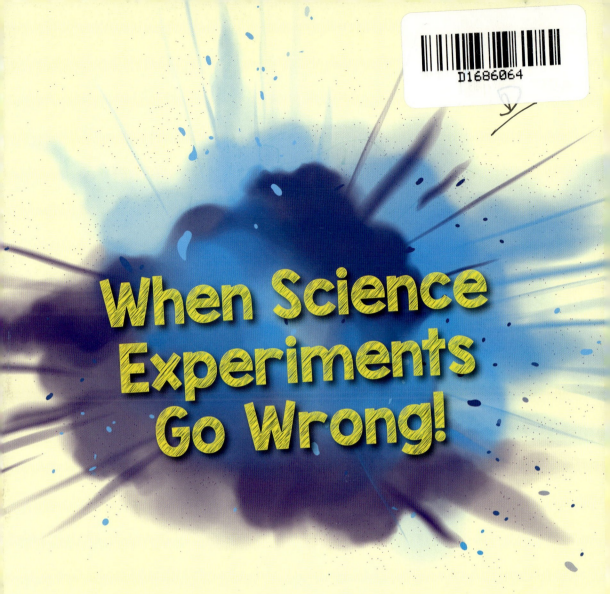

When Science Experiments Go Wrong!

Written by Isabel Thomas

Illustrated by Marcelo Badari

ISBN: 9781398324121

Text, Illustrations, design and layout © Hodder and Stoughton Ltd
First published in 2021 by Hodder & Stoughton Limited (for its Rising Stars
imprint, part of the Hodder Education Group),
An Hachette UK Company
Carmelite House, 50 Victoria Embankment, London EC4Y 0DZ
www.risingstars-uk.com

Impression number 10 9 8 7 6 5 4 3 2 1

Year 2025 2024 2023 2022 2021

Author: Isabel Thomas

Series Editor: Tony Bradman

Commissioning Editor: Hamish Baxter

Illustrator: Marcelo Badari/Bright International Group

Educational Reviewer: Helen Marron

Design concept and layouts: Lorraine Inglis Design

Editor: Amy Tyrer

With thanks to the schools that took part in the development of *Reading Planet KS2*, including: Ancaster CE Primary School, Ancaster; Downsway Primary School, Reading; Ferry Lane Primary School, London; Foxborough Primary School, Slough; Griffin Park Primary School, Blackburn; St Barnabas CE First & Middle School, Pershore; Tranmoor Primary School, Doncaster; and Wilton CE Primary School, Wilton.

The publishers would like to thank the following for permission to reproduce copyright material.

Cover, pp5, 13 © Yon Marsh/Alamy Stock Photo; cover, p4 © dule964/Adobe Stock; pp4, 22 © PikePicture/Adobe Stock; pp4–5, 6–7, 26–27, 36–37 © Grafth/Adobe Stock; pp5, 10 © Anton/Adobe Stock; pp5, 34 © Yomka/Adobe Stock; p7 © Avi Horovitz/Alamy Stock Photo; pp8–9, 18–19 © nik962/Adobe Stock; p8 © Nick Hanna/Alamy Stock Photo; p9 © frankenfotograf/Adobe Stock; p10–11 © striZh/Adobe Stock; p10 © Irinka/Adobe Stock; Elizabeth Tibbets; p11 © Alexey Kljatov/Adobe Stock; deZiGN/Adobe Stock; Alekss/Adobe Stock; pp12–13, 32–33 © amixstudio/Adobe Stock; p12 © JPC-PROD/Adobe Stock; p13 © INTERFOTO/Alamy Stock Photo; pp14–15, 22–23, 24–25, 34–35 © BAIVECTOR AdobeStock p14 © Juulijs/Adobe Stock; p15 © Science History Images/Alamy Stock Photo; pp16–17, 28–29 © alex_aldo AdobeStock p16 © richardseeley/Adobe Stock; Jo Varner/National Science Foundation; p17 © bruno ismael alves/Adobe Stock; Oren Sarid/Adobe Stock; p18 © Jamie Link/UCSD; Nikolay N. Antonov/Adobe Stock; p19 © Science Photo Library/Alamy Stock Photo; Annatamila/Adobe Stock; rost9/Adobe Stock; Evgeny/Adobe Stock; p20–21 © striZh/AdobeStock; p20 © Satjawat/Adobe Stock; p21 © Xinhua/Alamy Stock Photo; nechaevkon/Shutterstock; p23 © coffmancmu/Adobe Stock; p25 © Science History Images/Alamy Stock Photo; p26 © Joe Major/AP/Shutterstock; p27 © Monkey Business/Adobe Stock; p28 © Art Collection 2/Alamy Stock Photo; Giovanni Cancemi/Adobe Stock; p29 © Joseph von Mering/Wikimedia Commons; Oskar Minkowski/Wikimedia Commons; p30 © Vladimir Tretyakov/Shutterstock; michal812/Adobe Stock; p31 © Jtangosu/Wikimedia Commons; Ruslan Gilmanshin/Adobe Stock; Vandathai/Shutterstock; p32 © Science History Institute/Wikimedia Commons; Victor Metelskiy/Shutterstock; p33 © Olexandr/Adobe Stock; NASA Johnson/NASA; p34 © Science History Images/Alamy Stock Photo; p35 © RBM Vintage Images/Alamy Stock Photo; Everett Collection/Shutterstock; p36 © Marco Mayer/Adobe Stock; Nikolay/Adobe Stock; p37 © PJF Military Collection/Alamy Stock Photo.

MIX
Paper from responsible sources
FSC™ C104740
www.fsc.org

A catalogue record for this title is available from the British Library.

Printed in India.

Orders: Please contact Hachette UK Distribution, Hely Hutchinson Centre, Milton Road, Didcot, Oxfordshire, OX11 7HH.

Telephone: +44 (0)1235 400555. Email: primary@hachette.co.uk

Contents

Don't PANIC!

Science is an adventure. It's all about discovering new things.

Scientists start by asking questions. They choose questions that we don't yet know the answer to.

They might make **predictions**. This means saying what they *think* the answer could be.

Next, they design experiments to test their ideas. Sometimes their predictions are right. Sometimes they are wrong.

Scientists do not mind when experiments go wrong! It may mean they have discovered something exciting.

Scientists want to stay safe, even if an experiment ends up going wrong. Look out for these boxes to avoid danger and do science safely.

Some of the world's most important discoveries happened because something went wrong. Just ask Archimedes (say: *AR-ke-MEE-deez*). This Greek scientist was a genius. But he got stuck on a tricky problem.

The king asked Archimedes to work out if all of his crown was made of gold. Archimedes sat for weeks, puzzling over the question.

One day, Archimedes was enjoying a nice bath. But it was a bit too deep! When he lay down in the bath, water poured over the edge of the bathtub. This gave Archimedes an idea.

Archimedes realised that if he sank the king's crown in a bucket full of water, and measured how much water was pushed out of the bucket, it would help him work out how much gold was in the crown! His experiment helps to work out if objects such as ships will float or sink!

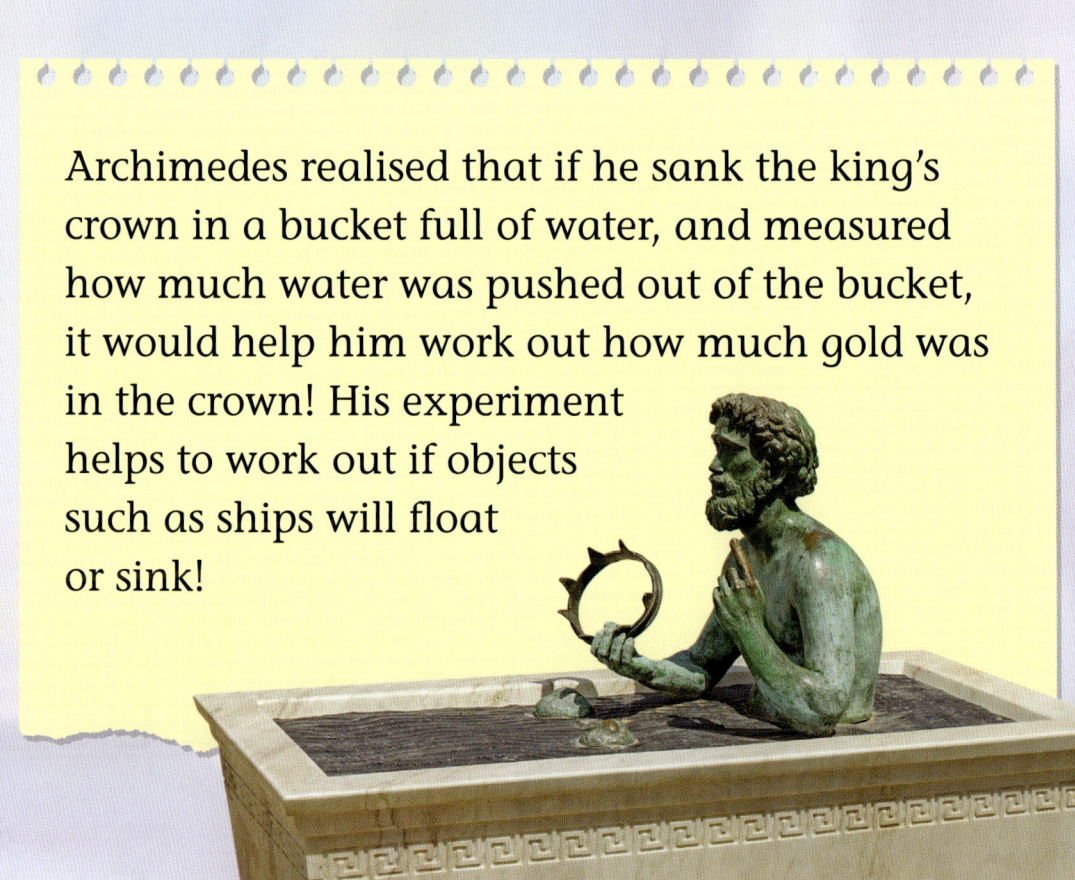

It is said that Archimedes jumped out of the bath and ran around naked shouting 'Eureka' (say: yor-EE-ka). This means 'I have found it!'. Don't do this next time you solve a maths problem!

This happened a long time ago, but scientists still learn a lot from mistakes, accidents and weird events!

A 'Tail' of DISASTER

Experiments can go wrong for *most people*. Even for the brainiest scientists in the world.

Isaac Newton was one of these scientists. 350 years ago, he had some new ideas about light. He did experiments to test his ideas. Isaac passed beams of sunlight through a special block of glass called a prism. He looked carefully at what happened and wrote everything down.

Isaac had been experimenting for weeks, when there was an accident. Isaac's pet dog, Diamond, knocked over a candle. It set fire to Isaac's desk. All his important notes burned to ash!

Poor Isaac could have cried! Perhaps he did. But he didn't give up.

One by one, Isaac repeated his experiments. He showed that sunlight is a mixture of every colour of light in a rainbow.

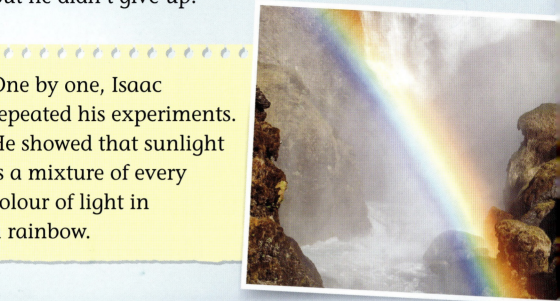

Isaac went on to have even better ideas! He wrote a book about motion, explaining how different forces cause things to move in different ways.

Isaac named the force that we call **gravity**. It helped him explain lots of weird things.

Why when you throw a ball up in the air, it falls back to Earth.

Why planets orbit the Sun.

Why candles topple when dogs knock them over!

Never leave a flame burning in a room unattended.

Missing MARKS

Not many people are excited to see a wasp. These insects are known for their nasty stings and they cause a commotion at picnics!

Elizabeth Tibbets disagrees. She thinks wasps are brilliant!

Elizabeth studies wasps, which like to live together in large groups called **colonies**. These wasps are known as **social** insects.

Each wasp in the group has certain jobs to do to help the colony survive.

How do insects with tiny brains organise themselves so well? Elizabeth wanted to know more. She planned to film a colony and track what each wasp did. To tell the wasps apart, she painted tiny marks on their backs.

Elizabeth Tibbets

As Elizabeth watched the film, she realised she had made a mistake. She had forgotten to mark some of the wasps! Her experiment had gone wrong … or had it?

Elizabeth saw that she could still tell the wasps apart by the patterns on their faces. She wondered if the wasps could do this, too.

Can you spot the difference?

Elizabeth designed a new experiment. This time, she painted the wasps to change the patterns on their faces. This caused confusion in the nest. It proved that Elizabeth's ideas were right!

A mistake had helped Elizabeth to discover something amazing.

Some people are allergic to wasp stings.

Mystery RECIPE

Sugar is delicious, but for some people it can be dangerous. People with diabetes cannot control the amount of sugar in their blood. Too much sugar can damage their body. People with diabetes check the amount of sugar in their blood to help them stay healthy.

This boy is learning how to measure his blood sugar using a special tool.

People with diabetes don't have to miss out on treats. There are special recipes that use **artificial** sweeteners. Sweeteners make food taste sweet without using sugar.

The first artificial sweetener was a **chemical** called saccharin (say: *SA-ka-rin*). It was discovered by accident!

It was 1879, and scientist Constantin Fahlberg (say: *FARL-berg*) had just got home from a long day in the **lab**. As Constantin tucked into his supper, he noticed that the food tasted strangely sweet. His hands and arms tasted sweet, too!

Constantin Fahlberg

Constantin went back to the lab and tasted EVERYTHING. He tracked down the sweet taste to a weak acid. This acid is hundreds of times sweeter than sugar, but our bodies can't digest it or use it for energy. Constantin named the acid saccharin, and he started selling it as an artificial sweetener.

!

Wash your hands well before you eat – wash them extra well after a science lesson.

Bad WEATHER

How do you discover something that humans can't see, hear, smell, feel or taste? Henri Becquerel (say: *ON-ree BECK-uh-rell*) did this thanks to an experiment that went wrong!

Henri Becquerel

Around 120 years ago, Henri was studying weird crystals that glowed in the dark.

We can see glowing light rays, but there are types of invisible rays that we can't see. Henri wondered if his crystals could give out invisible rays, too. To test this out, Henri designed an experiment using special paper.

"I will leave the crystals in sunlight. They will soak up sunlight energy and give out invisible rays. The rays will make a black mark on the special paper."

But the sun didn't come out for days. Henri's experiment seemed to be wrecked.

Henri still decided to look at the special paper and he saw something amazing.

There was a big black mark where the crystals had been! The crystals had given out invisible rays even when they hadn't soaked up sunlight energy.

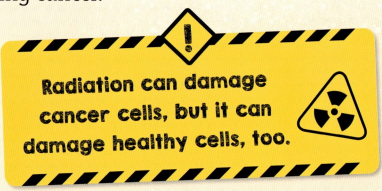

Actual marks on paper!

Next, Henri kept the crystals and the paper in the dark for a week. Once again, the crystals made black marks on the paper.

Henri had discovered a new ray called radiation. Today, we use radiation for lots of things, such as treating cancer.

Radiation can damage cancer cells, but it can damage healthy cells, too.

Forest FIRE

This cute creature is a pika (say: *PIE-ka*)!

Pikas are rodents, a bit like rabbits. They live in mountain forests and make dens in the cracks and gaps between boulders.

Jo Varner is an ecologist who studies pikas in the wild. She wants to find out how climate change affects pikas.

Jo Varner

Jo made **devices** to measure the temperature inside pika dens and find out how it changes over time. Jo put her devices inside the dens of two groups of pikas. One group lived low down in a river gorge. One group lived high up in Mount Hood National Forest.

But then, disaster struck …

When Jo came back to check her devices, she saw that a wildfire had destroyed 6000 acres of the forest. Jo burst into tears. She was sure the pikas must be dead, too.

However, Jo was amazed to find that her devices were still working. They showed her that the cracks and gaps between the boulders where the pikas lived had got no hotter than on a summer's day. Most pikas had survived!

Jo's experiment had not happened as she expected, but she had discovered something important. Pikas' den-building skills help them survive forest fires. It may help them to survive the effects of climate change, too.

Smashed TO DUST

Whoops! Have you ever broken something very important? This happened to Jamie Link. She turned the accident into a prize-winning invention!

Jamie was training to be a computer scientist. She was learning how to make **silicon** chips. These devices are inside every computer. They can be used to sense things, such as light or chemicals, too.

Jamie Link

Suddenly, there was a small explosion. The silicon chip crumbled into dust. Instead of clearing up the mess, Jamie looked closely.

Jamie noticed that the dust was still sensing things and sending signals. Each piece of dust was like a tiny version of the large chip!

Jamie called her invention 'smart dust'! In the future, it will be used to build digital devices as small as a grain of sand. They will be able to detect germs inside our bodies, or pollution in rivers, lakes and seas.

Jamie won a $50,000 prize for young inventors.

Don't Try This AT HOME

These scientists all did something very dangerous. They did experiments on themselves!

Almost blinded

Isaac Newton was supposed to be a genius but once did something very silly. He stared at the Sun with one eye open to see what would happen. His eyes did not work for weeks. He nearly went blind.

Killed by germs

Daniel Carrión wanted to find out what caused a mystery illness in Peru. He thought it might be germs. He gave himself an injection of the germs. Daniel was right – the germs did cause the illness; sadly, Daniel later died from the same illness.

! Never look directly at the Sun. It can damage your vision forever.

Nearly died

Barry Marshall wanted to see if germs living in our stomachs can sometimes cause disease. Barry decided to test his idea on himself. He 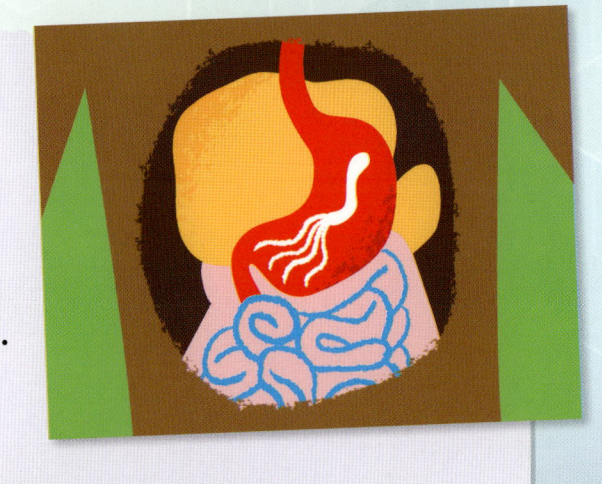 drank a cup of soup that had germs in it. He became very ill. Luckily, he survived. Barry's investigation has saved many lives. He even won the biggest prize in science – the Nobel prize.

Cured!

Tu Youyou (say: *TOO yoo-yoo*) wanted to find a cure for a deadly disease called malaria. She invented a new medicine. This could have been dangerous, so she tested the new medicine only on herself.

Tu Youyou

Today, Tu's medicine is the main cure for malaria. She won a Nobel prize, too.

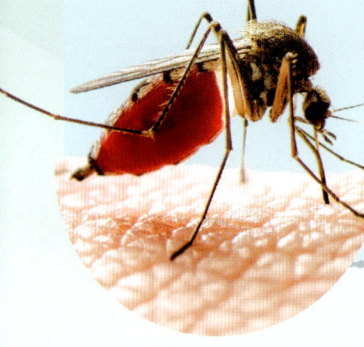

Broken GLASS

This is a story of how two wrongs made a right!
Scientists who work with chemicals use lots of glass.

tubes

beakers

flasks

✓ Glass does not soak up chemicals.
✓ It is see-through, so scientists can see what is happening inside.
✗ But glass is very fragile!

In 1903, when Édouard (say: *ED-waa*) Bénédictus knocked a glass flask off a shelf, he prepared himself for a SMASH!

Édouard opened his eyes, expecting to see a gigantic mess. He was shocked to see the pieces of broken glass were still stuck together in the shape of a flask!

Édouard rushed to the lab to find out why. He discovered that the flask was not completely empty. It hadn't been washed after an experiment and was coated in a thin layer of plastic. This had held the shattered glass together.

Édouard knew just how to use his discovery. In less than one day, Édouard invented shatterproof glass. Now his experiments involved breaking glass on purpose!

Édouard's mission was a success. Soon safety glass was being used in cars all around the world. It has saved millions of lives.

!

Broken safety glass can still give a nasty cut, so stay away from shattered glass.

Strange SOUNDS

Stars give out light and invisible rays, such as radio waves. Scientists detect radio waves with special telescopes, picking up signals from across the universe!

Robert Wilson and Arno Penzias (say: *pen-ZEE-as*) were listening to the signals collected by one of these radio telescopes. It was just like trying to tune a radio, except that the signals had been travelling for millions of years to get to Earth.

Robert and Arno kept hearing a weird buzzing sound. It seemed to be coming from every direction. They checked to see if the sound came from radios in nearby homes. They tried  removing some pigeons that had been pooping on the telescope. Nothing worked!

They solved the mystery when they realised the noise was coming from space itself! But not from a star or galaxy … They were hearing radio waves left over from the very beginning of the universe.

Robert Wilson and Arno Penzias

This was one of the most important discoveries ever. It is evidence that the universe began about 13.8 billion years ago with a big bang. Energy from the Big Bang is still zooming through space today, as radio waves.

The radio waves left over from the Big Bang are stronger in some parts of the universe. The discovery tells us that the universe is expanding – like a balloon being blown up.

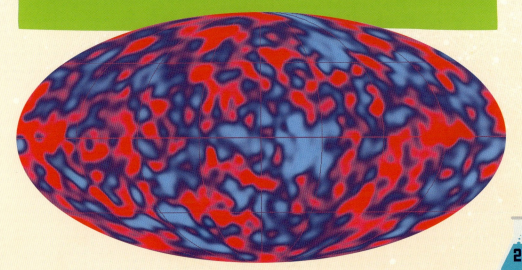

The Wrong PART

Building electrical devices can be hard. Electricians must be very careful. Wilson Greatbatch was an experienced inventor, but even he picked up the wrong part one day.

Wilson Greatbatch

Wilson was in his garage, building a device to count heartbeats. He wanted to measure the rhythm of a heart. But Wilson got it wrong. His device gave out tiny electrical signals instead of measuring them!

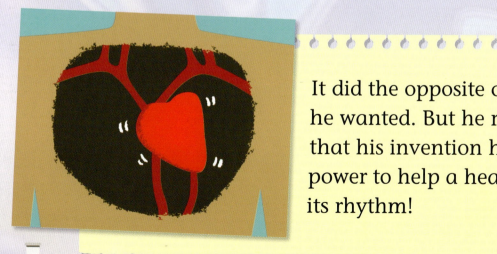

It did the opposite of what he wanted. But he realised that his invention had the power to help a heart keep its rhythm!

Wilson sprang into action. He turned his accidental invention into a tiny pacemaker device, so small that a person could wear it next to their heart.

The first pacemaker was fitted in 1960. Since then, pacemakers have helped millions of people to live healthy lives for longer.

pacemaker

Pacemakers are small devices with a battery. They send out tiny electrical signals in a rhythm. The signals help the person's heart stay healthy.

Wilson liked how his invention helps grandparents to have fun with their grandchildren. People with weaker hearts often don't get the right amount of oxygen to their brains, which slows them down.

UH OH!

Sometimes scientists are searching for one thing, but end up discovering something different. All sorts of things can be a clue – even a dog's wee!

Doctors and scientists have been puzzled by diabetes for thousands of years. Ancient Greek doctors noticed how the disease made people wee more than normal.

350 years ago, a British doctor called Thomas Willis noticed that his wee tasted sweet … yuck! Then, around 140 years ago, a weeing dog helped German scientists Joseph von Mering and Oskar Minkowski (say: *min-KOW-skee*) solve the mystery.

Never taste wee! Doctors did this hundreds of years ago because they didn't have tools to measure how much sugar is in wee.

Joseph and Oskar were trying to find out about an organ in the body called the pancreas. They gave a dog an operation to take out its pancreas. The next day, they noticed lots of flies around the dog's wee.

Joseph von Mering and Oskar Minkowski

This didn't happen to healthy dogs. They tested the wee and found it was full of sugar. This is a sign of diabetes. Joseph and Oskar had discovered that the pancreas was connected to diabetes.

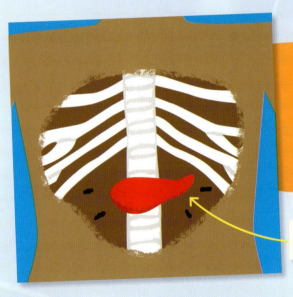

pancreas

Humans have a pancreas, too. It's part of our **gut**.

A healthy pancreas makes a substance that helps our bodies deal with sugar. Today, we can make this substance in a lab, and give it to people with diabetes so that they can lead healthy lives.

OVERBAKED!

Mas Subramanian (say: *SOO-bra-MAN-ee-an*) and his team were hunting for new materials to use in electronic devices.

They heated a mixture of **minerals** in a heater that was five times hotter than a kitchen oven.

They expected to see a pile of dark ash. But what came out was pure, bright, brilliant, beautiful blue!

Mas used to work for a lab that made paints and dyes. He knew it is rare to find blue minerals. He realised they had found something very special.

Colourful chemicals are called pigments. They named the new pigment YInMn blue. YInMn blue is not toxic and will not fade easily. It may be the perfect blue!

Since then, Mas and his team have been trying to invent more artificial pigments, from purple and turquoise to red.

Mas Subramanian

Too TOUGH?

Stephanie Kwolek (say: *kwoh-lek*) loved chemistry. She worked for one of the biggest labs in the world, making **synthetic** fabrics.

Stephanie Kwolek

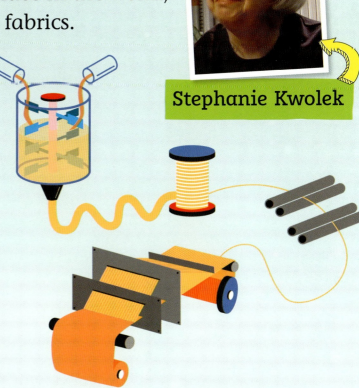

mixing chemicals

↓

spinning the mixture into threads

↓

weaving the threads into fabric

One day, Stephanie was looking for fibres that would stop car tyres from puncturing so easily. Some of her mixtures seemed to be going wrong. They were cloudy, instead of clear.

Some people might have thrown the mixtures away and started again. But not Stephanie. She made up her mind to keep trying to spin the mixtures into threads anyway.

To Stephanie's surprise, the threads were the strongest and stiffest that she'd ever seen. She used them to make fabric called Kevlar®, which is very light but is still five times stronger than steel!

Kevlar® is used to make protection for firefighters, scientists, astronauts and motorcyclists.

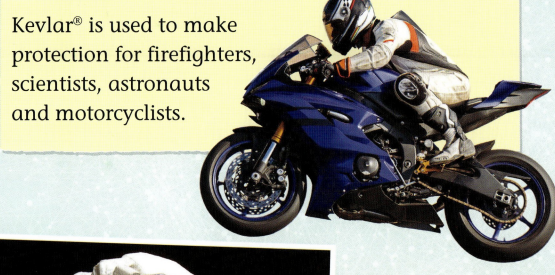

A layer of Kevlar® stops speeding space junk from making holes in spacesuits.

A Bug in THE SYSTEM

Lots of brilliant scientists start by making a mess!

As a child, Grace Hopper loved taking clocks apart to find out how they worked. By the time her parents noticed, she had wrecked eight clocks!

Grace Hopper

Make sure you ask before you take something apart. Grace got into trouble!

Grace got a job that let her play with machines. She became a computer scientist. She helped to build the world's first computers. They were much larger than today's computers.

Grace invented new ways to give computers instructions to tell them how to work.

One day, the computer stopped working. Grace took it apart. She found a dead moth trapped inside. Grace stuck the moth into her notebook. She said it was the first ever computer bug!

Actual page from Grace's notebook!

We still use the word 'bug' today to describe a problem with a computer. Computer bugs are not real insects – they are mistakes in the instructions that we give a computer.

Future MISTAKES

All these adventures prove that science is not just about getting things right.

It's about:

→ being curious
→ looking closely
→ coming up with ideas to explain what you see.

Many important discoveries were made by accident or chance. We can learn just as much from the things that go wrong as the things that go right!

Scientists don't worry about accidents and mistakes. They are just part of doing science. They are bumps on the road to great discoveries.

Maybe YOU will make some important mistakes in the future!

How scientists turn experiments that go wrong into SUCCESS:

1. Pay attention!
If you notice something weird, stop and look. It could be the start of a new discovery.

2. Read or watch a lot!
This helps your brain to make connections between the new things you notice and things that we know so far.

3. Share your ideas!
No one has *all* the right answers – not scientists, not parents, not even teachers! Don't be afraid to share your ideas, even if they are different.

Grace Hopper has some great advice.

A ship in port is safe; but that is not what ships are built for. Sail out to sea and do new things.

Glossary

artificial a human-made version of something that is found in nature

chemical a pure substance or a mixture of substances

colony a group of animals that live together

device a machine made to do a certain job

gravity the name for a force of attraction that pulls objects together

gut the collection of organs that break food down so that we can get to the energy and nutrients inside

lab short for laboratory, a room or building with special tools and equipment for scientists

mineral a substance that is found in nature

organ a part of a living thing that does a certain job, such as the heart or brain

prediction a best guess about what will happen in an experiment (or in the future)

silicon a substance used to make computer chips; it's the main building block of glass and sand, too!

silicon chip the part of a computer that processes information

social live together in an organised way

synthetic   made by humans; not found in nature

toxic   harmful to living things

Index

Chat about the book

1 Read page 11. How was Elizabeth Tibbets able to tell wasps apart?

2 Re-read pages 20 and 21. How are the scientists Barry Marshall and Tu Youyou similar?

3 How is a glossary useful?

4 Go back to page 23. Édouard Bénédictus rushed to the lab. What does this tell us?

5 Read page 27. Find a word that means the same as 'by mistake'.

6 Which scientist did you enjoy learning about the most? Why?